Los Angeles County Museum of Art

ART SPACES

William Hackman

SCALA

Los Angeles County Museum of Art

> The Los Angeles Museum of History, Science, and Art, in Exposition Park, 1914

The Los Angeles County Museum of Art, which opened in 1965, is the largest, most comprehensive art museum in the western United States. Its collections comprise more than one hundred thousand works of art—painting and sculpture, prints and drawings, decorative arts, costume and textiles, and photography—from every part of the world, dating from prehistory to the present day.

The museum is located in Hancock Park, on Wilshire Boulevard's Miracle Mile, midway between downtown Los Angeles and the Pacific Ocean. The Miracle Mile was first developed in the 1920s and 1930s as a retail district, an alternative to the increasingly crowded downtown, offering elegant shopping emporiums along a wide boulevard. The many department stores that dotted its landscape included some of the city's finest exemplars of pre–World War II architecture, including the 1929 art deco Bullocks Wilshire store, on the district's eastern edge, and the Streamline Moderne May Company, built a decade later along the western end. By the 1970s, high-rise office buildings had begun to replace the stores as the Miracle Mile fell victim to L.A.'s famously sprawling suburbs and their ever-expanding shopping malls. Wilshire Boulevard, however, remained the city's main artery.

Founding the Museum

Given the prominence of the city today as an international center of commerce and culture, it is a surprising fact that Los Angeles was without an art museum until the 1960s, when the Los Angeles County Museum of Art first opened its doors to the public. The city was a sparsely populated agricultural center until well into the twentieth century, with fewer people per square mile than many small and midsize towns in the Midwest and the South. Such a place was unlikely to have benefited from the country's first great boom of museum building, which began in the 1880s.

The first museum of any sort to be built in the area was the Los Angeles Museum of History, Science, and Art. Founded in 1910, it officially opened in November 1913 as part of a "jubilation" celebrating the completion of the aqueduct that would redirect water from the Owens Valley to the arid coastal plain of L.A. This original museum, located in Exposition Park near the University of Southern California, was built of brick and concrete (and remodeled in various styles over the next half century). The institution was primarily a museum of natural history; its first two directors were ornithologists. Art was, at best, an afterthought.

The first curator, Everett C. Maxwell, labored in vain to find enough art for the inaugural show. Legendary art critic and Art Institute of Chicago curator Katharine Kuh wrote in the *Saturday Review* that visitors "wandered through corridors of stuffed animals and scientific exhibits before encountering a work of art." According to Drew Cochran in

▲ The Mr. and Mrs. William Preston Harrison Gallery, in the rotunda of the Los Angeles Museum of History, Science, and Art, c. 1920

Los Angeles Magazine, even by 1954, when Richard (Ric) Brown arrived to head the museum's art division, he "found the art department an overcrowded and underqualified mess" and the museum "an historical anomaly—it was really a sixteenth-century *Wunderkammer,* with everything but a unicorn's head and an ostrich egg."

Until midcentury, many of the changing exhibitions mounted by the museum were in fact organized by local art groups. The California Water Color Society, for example, sponsored an annual show of its members' works, as did the Camera Pictorialists of Los Angeles.

The long struggle to establish an art museum in Los Angeles began with William Preston Harrison, an inveterate collector with catholic tastes. His brother had been instrumental in the early success of the Art Institute of Chicago, and when Preston, as he was known, arrived in L.A. in 1916, he decided he would do the same in his adopted hometown.

> *Portrait of William Preston Harrison* (1924), by Wayman Adams

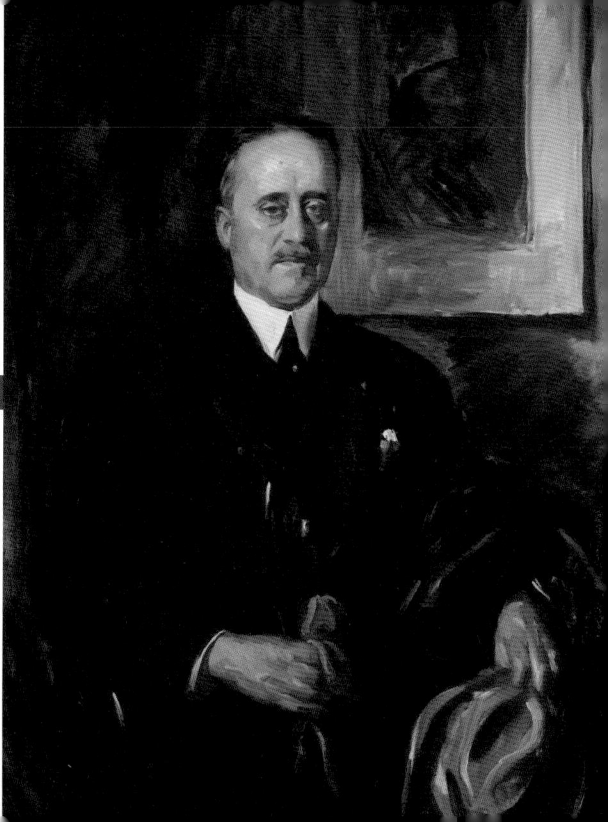

Harrison's arrival coincided with another singular event in the museum's history: the acquisition of ashcan school painter George Bellows's *Cliff Dwellers* (1913), the first work of art purchased by the institution. Just two years later, Harrison made his first gift of recent American paintings to the museum. He followed this less than a decade later with the first donations of modern French art, primarily paintings by artists then active in Paris. (Harrison included an unusual and farsighted provision for renewing both collections: they were to be reviewed periodically, and lesser works sold in order to buy others deemed superior.)

In 1946 James H. Breasted Jr., a professor of art history at UCLA, was named director of the museum. Just as important was the parallel appointment of William Valentiner as consultant to the director and de facto head of the art division. Valentiner had begun his career at the Kaiser-Friedrich Museum in Berlin and moved to the United States in the 1920s to become a curator at the Metropolitan Museum of Art, New York, and, later, director of the Detroit Institute of Arts. His impressive credentials were matched by his flair for charming potential donors. He guided many local collectors in assembling their collections and, in turn, encouraged their donations to the museum. Among these gifts were Edgar Degas's double portrait *The Bellelli Sisters* (1865–66) and Vincent van Gogh's ink-and-chalk portrait *The Postman Joseph Roulin* (1888).

▾ Portrait by Ludwig Meidner of William Valentiner, consultant to LACMA director James H. Breasted Jr.

No one was more charmed by Valentiner than William Randolph Hearst, the controversial newspaper baron who inspired Orson Welles's film *Citizen Kane*. Hearst, who had intended that his ranch at San Simeon eventually become a public museum of decorative arts, collected so prodigiously that his imports overwhelmed the U.S. Customs Service. From 1946 until his death five years later, Hearst was unstinting in his donations to the museum, becoming its greatest early benefactor and—in number of objects—still its most prolific. His contributions formed the basis for LACMA's holdings of Greek and Roman antiquities. Other gifts included nearly all of the museum's medieval and early Renaissance sculptures as well as a large number of paintings from the same periods, Islamic glass, Egyptian antiquities, Etruscan metalwork, and Renaissance tapestries. Hearst's beautiful French Renaissance Limoges enamels and extensive collection of Italian majolica are renowned components of LACMA's collection of European decorative arts. He also made possible the purchase of Giovanni Battista Piranesi's famous series of sixteen etchings, the *Carceri d'Invenzione* (c. 1761). His donations,

which laid the foundation on which a broad-ranging art museum could be formed, were crowded into the cluttered and outdated rooms of the all-purpose museum in Exposition Park.

> Ric Brown,
> LACMA director,
> 1961–66

Writing in the 1956 annual report to county supervisors, Ric Brown declared that it had "now reached a point where, from the standpoint of both permanent collections and changing exhibitions, simple increase is no longer desirable. Although the collections are by no means comprehensive nor, with some exceptions, as high in quality as they should be, the available space for display and storage is full." With this, Brown renewed the moribund effort to establish an art museum in Los Angeles.

His timing was good. In the decade following World War II, Los Angeles had grown into a very different place. The war had transformed the region's economy and set in motion changes that would ripple through society for years to come. The area's first freeways date to this era. Aerospace and electronics overtook agriculture as the primary industries, generating solidly middle-class jobs and drawing well-educated newcomers to settle in the proliferating suburbs. Returning veterans flooded the region's colleges and universities on the GI Bill. And with research funding from both business and government, the University of California rose in prominence to a level at which it could compete with the great private universities of the East and Midwest.

The postwar years ushered in a period of unprecedented energy and creativity in the L.A. art

> L.A. art scene personalities gather on LACMA stairs, 1968.

◄ Oil and tar fields in
the Miracle Mile
area, c. 1910

world. Artists who would become some of the most acclaimed and influential of the late twentieth century—Edward Kienholz, Robert Irwin, Bruce Nauman, and Edward Ruscha among them—were part of the city's artistic fabric in the 1950s and 1960s. And there was a growing community of collectors who were equal to the aesthetic challenges posed by these artists.

The postwar era also gave rise to a newly affluent middle class as well as a new generation of

wealthy individuals. It was from the ranks of these newly rich that Brown found two men who helped him realize his goal, Norton Simon and Edward W. Carter. Simon, who had built a small bottling operation into the Hunt Foods conglomerate, had not been collecting art for long, but he was well on his way to creating one of the finest collections of old masters assembled anywhere after World War II. Carter, who had built the country's first suburban shopping mall and guided the Broadway-Hale chain of department stores to regional dominance, already served on the boards of various civic organizations. More important, perhaps, was Carter's willingness to reach out to the more liberal residents of the city's Westside, among whom were several knowledgeable and innovative patrons and collectors who, until that time, had largely been excluded from the city's cultural establishment.

▲ The La Brea Tar Pits, with Howard Ball's popular mastodon sculpture and the Pavilion for Japanese Art

In 1958 the county of Los Angeles concluded contractual agreements with the board of trustees for a museum of art. A department dedicated to founding an art museum was established in 1961, and the county donated seven acres in Hancock Park—also home to the popular La Brea Tar Pits—as the site for the new museum.

Because of the tar pits, building on the site presented a formidable challenge. Archaeologists had to inspect the grounds for bones of prehistoric animals and give formal approval before excavation could get under way. Engineers had to pour a floating raft of concrete 3 feet thick and 200 feet long by 250 feet wide to lay the foundation. This was covered with soil, and the terrace and three steel-frame buildings were erected. *Time* magazine dubbed the institution the "temple on the tar pits."

Brown had proposed that the esteemed German modernist Ludwig Mies van der Rohe be named the new museum's architect, but the board opted for a local firm, William Pereira Associates. Pereira was one of Southern California's most sought-after architectural firms in the 1950s and 1960s, responsible for CBS's Television City; the University of California, Irvine, campus; and Los Angeles International Airport. Its major national commissions included the launch facility at Cape Canaveral and the iconic Transamerica Pyramid in San Francisco.

Pereira's design for the museum wedded mid-twentieth-century modernism to neoclassical elements, a style found in much civic architecture of the time. Lincoln Center, in New York, and the Los Angeles Music Center were contemporaneous examples. The LACMA

▲ Plaza fountains at night, c. 1965

◄ The Ahmanson
Building's three-
story central atrium

➤ Ahmanson Building
galleries, late 1960s

Displayed in the Ahmanson Building, LACMA's collection of South and Southeast Asian art is world renowned.

In 2003, in conjunction with *The Circle of Bliss: Buddhist Meditational Art*, Tibetan Buddhist monks created a sand mandala in the Ahmanson Atrium.

Chinese and Korean galleries in the Ahmanson Building, late 1990s

➤ *Soap Bubbles*
(1733–34), by Jean-
Siméon Chardin, was a
gift of the Ahmanson
Foundation.

◄ Architect's sketch of the Lytton Gallery (later renamed the Hammer Building), c. 1964

◄ Installation view, *The American Discovery of Ancient Egypt*, Hammer Building galleries, 1995

plan, similar to that of Lincoln Center and the Music Center, featured three pavilions set in a plaza that was elevated and removed from the street. "The museum is eminently suited to the climate and landscape of Southern California," Katharine Kuh wrote in the *Saturday Review*. "On one side it faces a dynamic city; on the other, light-struck mountains and luxurious vegetation."

On the west side of the plaza, the four-level Ahmanson Building, named for Howard F. Ahmanson, one of the museum's first and most generous benefactors, rose 85 feet. Its galleries were laid out around a 60-foot-square atrium that opened to a roof skylight, which filled the building's interior with natural light. Much of LACMA's permanent collection has found its home here.

On the plaza's north side was the Lytton Gallery, named for museum benefactor Barton Lytton (and renamed the Frances and Armand Hammer Building in 1968), which housed temporary and loan exhibitions. The fifteen-and-a-half-foot-high ceiling on its first floor was designed as a grid of tracks to which temporary modular partitions could be affixed, making it easy to reconfigure the space to meet the particular requirements of an exhibition. Floor-to-ceiling windows opened the gallery to northern light as well as to a view of the surrounding park and, in the near distance, the Hollywood Hills.

The third pavilion, the Leo S. Bing Center, named for benefactor Anna Bing Arnold's late husband, included the 600-seat auditorium that continues to serve as the primary venue for the numerous lecture,

> *The Candied House*, a play by Jack Larsen, performed in the Leo S. Bing Theater, 1966

> Robert Rauschenberg dance performance, Leo S. Bing Theater, 1966

film, and music series essential to the museum's public programming. In its first two years, the museum realized an annual attendance of 300,000 at the nearly 400 events it presented. One of the museum's first efforts in this direction was providing a permanent home to the internationally acclaimed Monday Evening Concerts, which had led an itinerant existence since its founding in 1939 and which became an L.A. mainstay due to the efforts of its longtime director, Dorrance Stalvey. From the Bing Center's lobby, visitors also could enter the museum's cafeteria, with a view to the eastern edge of Hancock Park and the La Brea Tar Pits.

The plaza was punctuated by sculpture groups and landscaped areas immediately north of the Ahmanson Building. Surrounding the plaza and the

The LACMA campus, situated in Hancock Park, 1965

rough-hewn marble buildings were reflecting pools with fountains. "The gleaming white buildings appear as enormous jewels set in a placid blue frame," read a *Los Angeles Times* photo caption. To reach the plaza, visitors traversed a wide ramp and bridges over the pools, arriving at the founders' wall, flanked by a pair of grand stairways. A large fountain and an abstract sculpture formed a centerpiece to the causeway across the pools, but works by David Smith and Alexander Calder—the latter created the large and playful mobile *Hello Girls*—were the real highlights. "What with the splashing of the water and its drumming against the metal plates of the mobiles," declared *New York Times* critic John Canaday, "the fountain is as delightful audibly as it is visually."

In its first few years, LACMA presented a slate of exhibitions worthy of the finest museums in the country. For the first time, L.A. audiences were able to see large traveling shows, such as *7000 Years of Iranian Art*, organized by the

▲ Workers installing
one of David Smith's
Cubi sculptures in a
reflecting pool, 1965

➤ Alexander Calder
overseeing the
installation of his
mobile sculpture
Hello Girls, 1965

Smithsonian Institution, and *Alberto Giacometti*, which came from the Museum of Modern Art, New York.

LACMA also organized major exhibitions of its own, a remarkable achievement for a museum still in its infancy. The opening show, a survey of the works of postimpressionist Pierre Bonnard, was followed in short order by an extraordinary series of landmark exhibitions developed by modern art curator Maurice Tuchman, including *New York School: The First Generation, Paintings of the 1940s and 1950s* and *American Sculpture of the Sixties*. Critic Jules Langsner was guest curator for LACMA's retrospective of Man Ray's work, in 1966. And a number of younger artists who eventually gained international stature had their first solo museum

> ➤ LACMA curators periodically have mounted small exhibitions—such as this 1987 display of Eames furniture—at the Pacific Design Center in West Hollywood.

exhibitions at LACMA during this period, among them Robert Irwin, R. B. Kitaj, John Mason, Kenneth Price, and Peter Voulkos.

These exhibitions drew large and enthusiastic crowds. Nearly 5 million visitors passed through LACMA's galleries the first two years, outpacing all museums except New York's Metropolitan Museum of Art. Membership grew to more than thirty thousand. The national press was equally welcoming. Under the headline "Culture Way Out West," Canaday wrote that while the youthful LACMA still had "a long distance to go before it can be in a class with the great ones of this country . . . one gets the impression that Los Angeles will not be content until it is done."

> Earl A.
> Powell III,
> LACMA director,
> 1980–92

> Wilshire
> Boulevard view
> of the Robert O.
> Anderson
> Building, 1986

D.C., brought in the New York firm of Hardy Holzman Pfeiffer Associates (HHPA, which recently had completed award-winning projects for the St. Louis Art Museum and the Cooper-Hewitt Museum, the Smithsonian Institution's National Design Museum) to develop a new master plan for the LACMA campus. The resulting three-phase proposal set in motion changes that ultimately transformed the museum.

The cornerstone for those changes was the dramatic four-story Robert O. Anderson Building fronting Wilshire Boulevard. This represented a radical reimagining of LACMA: "We were bursting at the seams," Powell explained, "so we turned the whole

A new chapter in LACMA's history began in 1980 with the arrival of Earl A. ("Rusty") Powell III as director. Shortly after taking office, Powell, formerly senior curator at the National Gallery of Art in Washington,

◄ Friday Night Jazz on the Los Angeles Times Central Court

▲ Wilshire Boulevard view of the Robert O. Anderson Building, 1986

museum . . . inside out." The original concept of pavilions in a plaza gave way to a complex that was an integral part of a bustling urban environment. The classically scaled, colonnaded pavilions were largely obscured by the monumental limestone edifice that now greeted the sidewalk.

The building rose one hundred feet above Wilshire Boulevard. Its otherwise imposing stone facade was softened by horizontal rows of glass brick alternating with glazed bands of green terracotta that ran the length of the building on the Wilshire side. Reviewers also noted the building's theatricality and evocation of classic Hollywood glamour.

From the sidewalk, visitors passed through the five-story-high entrance and up a twenty-foot-wide stairway, bordered by a cascading fountain, to the central court. Powell considered this plaza "the architectural, visual, and symbolic focus of the entire

> The Iris and
> B. Gerald Cantor
> Sculpture Garden

museum complex, and a major public space for Los Angeles." The plaza has been a popular spot for concerts (particularly the longtime city favorite Friday Night Jazz) and is immediately surrounded by a restaurant and shop, in addition to the art galleries.

Perhaps the most assertive gesture in HHPA's response to the museum's original layout was the new wing's west wall, which jutted toward the Ahmanson Building at a forty-five-degree angle,

> *Monument to
> Honoré de Balzac*
> (modeled 1897),
> one of a grouping
> of Rodin sculp-
> tures in the Iris
> and B. Gerald
> Cantor Sculpture
> Garden

stepped down at each level, producing an outdoor space set slightly apart from the main plaza. Descending a set of stairs running parallel to Wilshire Boulevard below, visitors were led into the Iris and B. Gerald Cantor Sculpture Garden, which, inaugurated in 1989, contained several works by Auguste Rodin, including the massive *Monument to Honoré de Balzac* (modeled 1897).

At plaza level, the new Anderson Building offered about eighteen thousand square feet for temporary exhibitions. The upper-floor permanent-collection galleries were based on the beaux arts concept of the enfilade, a sequence of galleries offering clear directional vistas.

▲ David Hockney in front of *Mulholland Drive: The Road to the Studio* (1980), at his 1988 retrospective

▲ The 2003 *Erté/Opera & Ballets Russes/Dance* exhibition featured rare costumes and drawings from LACMA's collections.

➤ *L'Esprit Nouveau: Purism in Paris, 1918–1925* (2001) showcased a movement that embraced painting and architecture. This is a detail of LACMA's re-creation of Le Corbusier's Pavilion de l'Esprit Nouveau at the 1925 International Exposition of Modern Decorative and Industrial Arts, in Paris.

> Pavilion for
> Japanese
> Art under
> construction,
> 1988

> Bruce Goff's Pavilion
> for Japanese Art

"There is simply nothing like it anywhere," wrote Christopher Knight in the *Los Angeles Herald-Examiner* when the Pavilion for Japanese Art opened in 1988. LACMA's new building was, indeed, unique. It was the first time an American encyclopedic museum had dedicated a separate building to house and exhibit Japanese art; it also was the first in the Western world to show Japanese art as it was meant to be seen. Above all, however, Knight's observation was a reference to the building's exterior. With its dramatic, sweeping curves and flagstone cylinders, the Pavilion, according to Knight, resembled "some mutant offspring of a great four-masted schooner and the Starship Enterprise that has just slid into its berth."

Such reactions were typical. Most reviewers, like the general public, found the building bizarre yet somehow "right." *Los Angeles Times* architecture critic Sam Hall Kaplan thought the building seemed to rise "out of the La Brea Tar Pits like a pterodactyl perched on a sinuous space station." It was, he added approvingly, "like one of those wonderful overwrought warrior helmets, replete with horns and animals' ears that were worn by the ancient shogunate samurai." Paul Goldberger, in a

New York Times review, found "its strangeness . . . is not that overwhelming" but rather "endearing, almost sweet."

Designed by Bruce Goff, who was known for his extravagant and eccentric architectural designs, the Pavilion houses the museum's collection of Japanese works, which date from around 3000 BC to the present day. At its heart is the renowned Shin'enkan Collection of paintings assembled by Goff's long-standing patron, Joe D. Price. Price developed an interest in Japanese art and culture as a young man while working with Frank Lloyd Wright. Wright had been commissioned by Price's father, Harold C. Price, to design an office tower in the family's hometown of Bartlesville, Oklahoma. The younger Price spent thirty years assembling the Shin'enkan Collection, which is widely regarded as the finest collection of Edo-period painting outside Asia. The Price donation comprises more than three hundred painted scrolls and screens. A key condition of his gift was that the museum build the Pavilion according to the design sketched out by Goff, who died in 1982.

Most Western museums display screens as they would easel paintings: flat against a wall. The Pavilion's east wing was designed to approximate as closely as possible the viewing context assumed by eighteenth- and nineteenth-century artists and patrons. The works are displayed in *tokonoma*, alcoves that permit viewers to contemplate each one in relative isolation. "The art is to be experienced, not studied," Price emphasized. The *tokonoma* are set off to the sides of a spiraling ramp that winds gently down through the open space of the gallery. Goff's plan called for visitors to ride an elevator to the top and stroll down the ramp to view the art, just as in the Wright-designed Solomon R. Guggenheim Museum in New York. "It is a marvelous room," Goldberger noted, "at once energetic and serene."

The *Los Angeles Times*'s Kaplan agreed. The Pavilion, he wrote, "appears to work magnificently for both the art and the viewer." He concluded: "Here is a building that may not please popular taste, or coalesce the LACMA complex, but it is a pleasure to visit."

◄ ► Interior views, Pavilion for Japanese Art

Moving West, 1995

As the region's department stores went out of business or were absorbed by national chains, the elegant buildings that lined Wilshire Boulevard were closed or converted. The May Company was among the last to go, shuttering its store at the corner of Fairfax Avenue in 1988. Built in 1939, the five-story building was designed by Albert C. Martin Sr. and Samuel A. Marx (Martin also collaborated on such local landmarks as downtown's Million Dollar Theater and Los Angeles City Hall). The building is one of the best examples of modernist commercial architecture in Los Angeles, epitomizing the transition from Zigzag Moderne to International Style. It has long been admired in particular for the distinctive gold column framed by black Vitrolite glass that rises like a giant lipstick tube above the store's southwest corner. It sat empty, its future uncertain, until the museum's trustees acquired it in 1995 and transformed it into LACMA West, a new space for exhibitions as well as staff offices.

About four thousand square feet of the refurbished building was given over to the Bernard and Edith Lewin Galleries for Latin American Art, established when the museum acquired the Lewin collection in 1997. Additional galleries have housed several popular traveling shows, including *Van Gogh's Van Goghs*, in 1999, and *Tutankhamun and the Golden Age of the Pharaohs*, in 2005.

The other main exhibition space on the ground floor of LACMA West is the Boone Children's Gallery, home to special exhibitions, often experimental and always interactive, designed to engage young visitors. Through its LACMA Lab, it commissioned numerous Los Angeles–area artists to develop

In 1995 museum trustees acquired the empty May Company building, which became LACMA West.

interactive installations, often involving new media and technologies.

As part of the second phase in LACMA's current expansion, LACMA West will continue to be a center for experimentation and education, for both children and adults. In addition, it will house a new restaurant and bookstore, as well as staff and administrative offices.

In 2006 LACMA acquired a West L.A. office designed by influential Southern California architect John Lautner, a protégé of Frank Lloyd Wright best known for his residential work. The office—which combines walls of copper and glass, a slate floor, and a hardwood ceiling—was designed by Lautner for a local businessman in 1987. Current plans call for it to be installed on the top floor of LACMA West.

- In 1998, for the retrospective *Love Forever: Yayoi Kusama, 1958–1968*, the artist installed hundreds of mirrored globes on the LACMA West Green.

- Artist Allan Kaprow and his eleven-year-old son, Bram Crane-Kaprow, created *No Rules Except . . . ?*, a room in the exhibition *Made in California: NOW*, Boone Children's Gallery, LACMA West, 2000.

- Los Carpinteros, a collaborative group of Cuban artists, erected *Transportable City* on the LACMA West Green, 2001.

- Installation view of *Nano*, an interactive exhibition developed by the LACMA Lab educational initiative, Boone Children's Gallery, LACMA West, 2003

Renzo Piano and BCAM, 2007

> Andrea L. Rich,
> LACMA president
> and director,
> 1995–2005

former vice-chancellor at UCLA who assumed the post of LACMA president in 1995, Rich sought to build the museum's collections in ways that addressed not only the strengths and weaknesses of the holdings but also the rapidly changing character of the city of Los Angeles.

The demographic patterns that had defined Los Angeles during the postwar boom changed dramatically in the 1980s and 1990s. Immigration, especially from Asia and Latin America, was forging the most ethnically diverse metropolis in the world, and the county's population was climbing rapidly toward today's 10 million mark. Simultaneously, the area was growing into an international capital of contemporary art, home to some of the country's most influential artists and active collectors, as well as younger artists, many of whom were drawn to the city's unparalleled number of outstanding art schools. The number of galleries also had mushroomed; a half dozen gallery

LACMA today comprises seven buildings stretched along nearly one-third of a mile of Wilshire Boulevard in thirty-three-acre Hancock Park. The present configuration dates to the mid-1990s and the blueprint for expansion first drawn up by the institution's president and director at the time, Andrea L. Rich. A

▲ Installation view, *Made in
California: Art, Image, and
Identity, 1900–2000*, 2000

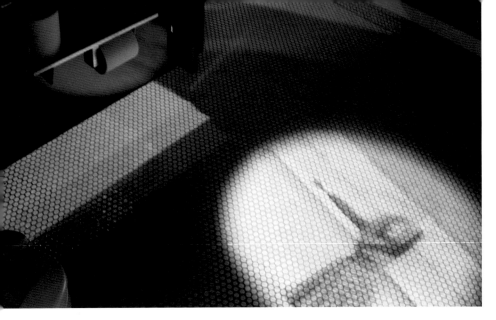

▲ *Contemporary Projects 4: New Sitings* (2000) dispensed
with the traditional display of objects in segregated
gallery spaces. This video installation by Pipilotti Rist was
placed in a restroom in the Pavilion for Japanese Art.

▾ Paintings by Margaret Kilgallen in the old LACMA parking garage. Artists were invited to create murals in the garage as part of the 2000 *Made in California* exhibition.

▲ LACMA's Institute for Art and Cultures presented artists Komar and Melamid's Asian Elephant Art and Conservation Project in 2000.

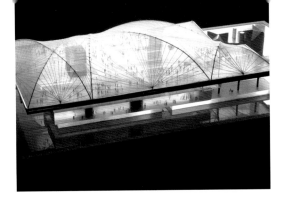

▲ Model by Rem Koolhaas,
winner of LACMA's 2002
architectural-design
competition

➤ *On Tour with Renzo
Piano & Building
Workshop*, Ahmanson
Atrium, 2005

districts flourished in neighborhoods from downtown to Santa Monica.

Under Rich's guidance, LACMA expanded on several fronts. First, it moved aggressively to strengthen the diversity of its holdings—in particular, Latin American, Asian, and Islamic art—reflecting the region's multiethnic character. In the millennium year, LACMA initiated a plan to reconsider its physical campus in light of its evolving collections and the changing character of Los Angeles, a world art capital in the era of global cultural and economic exchange. The museum commissioned studies from internationally celebrated architects, among them a 2002 proposal by Rem Koolhaas that included tearing down all the existing buildings, with the exceptions of the Pavilion for Japanese Art and LACMA West. It was a daring and inventive proposal, but it proved both controversial and prohibitively expensive, and the plan was dropped in 2004.

Trustee Eli Broad then stepped forward with an alternative plan: he would fund a new building, the Broad Contemporary Art Museum (BCAM), as part of LACMA, to house both his own well-known collection of contemporary art and the museum's. Rich described Broad's offer as "a strategic gift in a giant puzzle."

Businessman Broad and his wife, Edythe, leading philanthropists in the United States, support important initiatives in education and medical research, and they have been especially active in promoting the arts in Los Angeles. Broad was the founding chairman of the board of trustees of L.A.'s Museum of Contemporary Art as well as a driving force in raising the funds to complete the Frank Gehry–designed Walt Disney Concert Hall. The Broads began collecting contemporary art in 1969. Fifteen years later, they established the Broad Art Foundation, an innovative "lending library" that makes its holdings available to museums and university galleries around the world. The couple's own collection was the subject of an exhibition that traveled around the United States and to Europe from 2001 to 2003.

An architectural plan by Renzo Piano was approved for the Broad building in 2005. Piano, the

> Centre Pompidou, Paris

> Menil Collection, Houston

> Beyeler Foundation, Basel

1998 Pritzker Architecture Prize laureate, is a designer whose buildings are embraced with equal enthusiasm by both critics and the general public. His many museum buildings in particular have garnered singular praise. In 1974, with partner Richard Rogers, Piano designed the Centre Pompidou, in Paris. The project thrust the two young designers, relative unknowns at the time, into the international spotlight. In the years since, Piano has been responsible for several highly acclaimed museum designs and additions in the United States and Europe—the Menil Collection, in Houston (1986), the Beyeler Foundation museum, in Basel, Switzerland (1997), and extensions to the High Museum of Art, in Atlanta (2005), and the Morgan Library and Museum, in New York (2006), among them.

At LACMA, Piano was presented with twin challenges: first, a building for BCAM; second, a master plan that would reconcile the campus's disparate architectural elements and provide a template for future expansion.

The BCAM building was a relatively straightforward matter for a master builder such as Piano. (Because of the tar pits, however, there were obstacles similar to those encountered nearly a half century earlier when the museum's original buildings were constructed, and archaeologists once again were onsite for inspection and approval.) The travertine-clad BCAM—its two identical three-story wings joined by a narrower midsection—provides 60,000 square feet of exhibition space. Piano's scheme placed all the structural support for the building in its outer walls, thereby creating an interior free of bearing walls or columns. The resulting loftlike galleries thus can be configured entirely according to the requirements of the art on view. With their high ceilings—20 feet on the ground and third floors, 18 feet on the second—the galleries can accommodate the often enormous creations of many contemporary artists.

Piano's reputation is founded in part on his ability to create spaces that seem almost to be composed of light. The top floor of BCAM is a case in point. The building is crowned by an elaborate system of filtered skylights and louvers that admit abundant daylight into the third-floor galleries. The roof is composed of three layers of glass imprinted with a synthetic coating that blocks ultraviolet rays. The steel structure above the roof consists of twenty south-facing angled panels. This permits indirect light from the north to penetrate but blocks the direct southern light—which in Southern California is harsh as well as hot—that can damage works of art.

A bright red steel-framed escalator angles across the building's north side and provides the main approach to the building, on its third floor. The covered, girderlike apparatus also includes a triple-tiered stairway. Nicknamed the "spider" for its long-legged appearance, the structure is one of the most distinctive architectural features of the new LACMA, evoking at once a nineteenth-century ironworks and Piano's famous exterior access to the Centre Pompidou. Visitors also can ride the room-size elevator in the building's center section, which is glassed in from top to bottom.

The greater challenge facing Piano was integrating the varied architectural styles of LACMA's existing buildings to make traversing the sprawling campus a cohesive experience for the visitor. His first step was to shift the museum's center of gravity to the new BP Grand Entrance along the former Ogden Drive. Approached by walkways from both Wilshire Boulevard and Sixth Street, as well as by elevator from the new underground parking garage, the ninety-by-ninety-foot entrance is equipped with overhead solar panels. The entrance, which includes information and ticketing booths, is a central hub with spokes that radiate along one axis to the

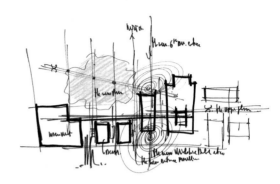

> An early sketch by Renzo Piano of his plan to integrate the LACMA campus

▼ Wilshire Boulevard elevation showing BCAM and the BP Grand Entrance

museum's galleries and, along the other, to Hancock Park and the surrounding streets.

A canopy of the same bright red steel beams that enclose the "spider" covers the Pavilion's roof and the corridor that extends from LACMA West, at one end, to the Ahmanson Building Atrium, at the other, unifying the string of buildings both physically and visually. Piano cited the experience of strolling through the streets of small European towns as a precedent: "In a short walk, you may find many surprises—a church, a piazza, a palazzo." Similarly, at LACMA, one encounters buildings from different periods, each opening to a new kind of surprise.

▲ Renzo Piano BCAM model, 2006

➤ Construction of the "spider,"
north face of BCAM, 2007

> Michael Govan,
  named LACMA
  CEO and Wallis
  Annenberg
  Director in 2006

> Installation view,
  *Dan Flavin: A
  Retrospective*,
  2007

When Michael Govan was named LACMA's director and chief executive officer in 2006, he approached Renzo Piano with a proposal that placed works of art front and center. As deputy director of the Solomon R. Guggenheim Museum and, later, director of the Dia Art Foundation, Govan has devoted much of his professional life to working closely with artists, including Donald Judd and Dan Flavin, among many others, and creating institutions that challenge the traditional relationship between art and architecture. He has established a similarly ambitious agenda for reinventing LACMA, enlisting Piano to design another building, for temporary exhibitions—funded in part by trustee Lynda Resnick and her husband, Stewart—and commissioning works by some of today's best-known artists.

For Dia's thirty-one-acre exhibition park on the banks of the Hudson River in Beacon, New York, which opened to international acclaim in 2003,

‹ Robert Irwin drawing of
  concept for palm garden

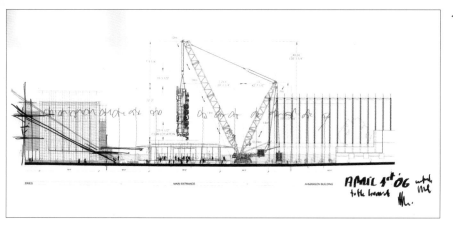

Govan collaborated with artist Robert Irwin to con-
vert the former Nabisco box-printing facility and
grounds into a unique indoor-outdoor space for
experiencing art. It seemed only natural, then, that
he would once again turn to Irwin, an artist who has
been identified with Los Angeles since he first came
to international prominence for his "light and space"
works in the 1960s. For LACMA, Irwin designed a

palm garden based on the structural grid of the campus's most recent additions.

Works by other artists will be installed
throughout the campus. Michael Heizer's *Levitated
Mass*, which will anchor the northwest corner of the
park, is a 25-foot-high granite boulder that appears
to float over a passageway incised into the earth.
Chris Burden's *Urban Light* comprises close to two

> Detail of salvaged
> street lamps that
> will be part of
> Chris Burden's
> *Urban Light*
> installation

hundred vintage Los Angeles streetlights collected by the artist and carefully refurbished with a uniform finish. "It is a perfect, glowing sculpture for the park," Govan says. Feasibility and engineering studies also are under way for *Train*, by Jeff Koons. The work, featuring a 70-foot locomotive dangling above the sidewalk from a 160-foot crane, will greet visitors as they approach the BP Grand Entrance from Wilshire.

Not all the large sculpture installations are outdoors. Moving east from the entrance to the Ahmanson Building, visitors enter at street level, in the well of the building's atrium. Here they encounter Tony Smith's enormous sculpture *Smoke* (1967), which, at 24 feet high and 48 feet long, is one of the largest works ever conceived by an American artist. Despite *Smoke*'s complex geometry and monumental scale, art historian Robert Storr likened it to "the skeleton of a cloud." Smith appeared next to the work on the cover of *Time* in 1967, when a wooden mock-up of *Smoke* (described in the magazine as "its own hypnotic environment, like some underwater coral growth") was installed in the inner courtyard of the Corcoran Gallery of Art, in Washington, D.C., the only other time any version of the work has been exhibited.

Michael Govan hopes that involving contemporary artists in LACMA's architectural transformation—to create environments within and focus the spaces around the buildings—will bring a fresh energy to the newly integrated museum campus. "A point of view can be created here, starting from where we are in the world," he explained. "It's not just about building buildings. It requires coordinating a worldview and a viewpoint.

"The content of the museum should reflect that our community is Wilshire Boulevard, the county of Los Angeles, the state of California, and the western United States. Our community emerges culturally from the wide-open spaces of the West, from our relationship to Latin America and Asia. We have to broaden our horizons to reflect that."

Ultimately, Govan is setting the stage for LACMA's future. The current phase of metamorphosis

is simply clearing the ground or, as he put it: "priming the canvas by clarifying the site. Once we have done that with the new building, and its generosity of space for contemporary art, our obligation is to do that for the whole history of art."

▲ The boulder for Michael Heizer's *Levitated Mass*